SELDO̶ ̶ ̶ ̶D

THE HOME PLACE

For Thomas,
best of traveling companions.

Contents

seldom seen road

poems

JENNA BUTLER

NeWest Press

COPYRIGHT © JENNA BUTLER 2013

LIBRARY AND ARCHIVES CANADA CATALOGUING IN PUBLICATION
Butler, Jenna, 1980–
Seldom seen road / Jenna Butler.
Poems. ISBN 978-1-927063-31-6
I. Title.
PS8603.U84S44 2013   C811'.6   C2012-906586-2

Editor for the Board: Douglas Barbour
Cover and interior design: Natalie Olsen, Kisscut Design
Author photo: Thomas Lock

   Canadian Heritage Patrimoine canadien

NeWest Press acknowledges the financial support of the Alberta
Multimedia Development Fund and the Edmonton Arts Council
for our publishing program. We further acknowledge the financial
support of the Government of Canada through the Canada Book
Fund (CBF) for our publishing activities. We acknowledge the sup-
port of the Canada Council for the Arts which last year invested
$24.3 million in writing and publishing throughout Canada.

#201, 8540–109 Street
Edmonton, Alberta T6G 1E6
780.432.9427
NeWest Press www.newestpress.com

No bison were harmed in the making of this book.
printed and bound in Canada 1 2 3 4 5 13 12

inbound

Inbound

ten thousand miles
   a pillar clock &
   sterling tea service

& here   the wagon spreads you
like grains of sand   or salt
look back all you want
   one cart track ambling
   mercurial skyline

winter ballast   dim
shaggy banks of snow
soddy's blue clay walls
frosted through   & you
so much better for
a silver service
sans tea

Roots

you saved the onion sets
for february   the chinook's
sentinel line standing off
across the poplars
     rubbed those snubnosed bulbs
     free of peatmoss   sawdust
somehow the thin   green tips
arcing across the kitchen table
& you always knew

how you tasted
soil from a bare palm
planting out the cutting garden
sweet or   sour
& what to plant
how   those thick roots lounged
prehensile   succulent
in September earth

what was it you were learning
     that soil against your tongue &
     your knotted hands
     battling wild cucumber vine
     cutworms   midwinter frost
what word for yourself in   this
capricious geography
this arbitrary landscape

Victory Garden

mint

best picked fresh &
slightly damp   thin air dawn
garden standing sodden

this taken in
tea   to be drunk only in
sunlight   preferably bright
never alone

reminds us of
roots   white &
blind   furred grope of
vegetative sinew
menacing as   memory

possibly invasive
bears watching

bergamot

you will have to fight off
the bees

static midsummer heat   the border
redolent with oranges & spice
iridescent pinwheels of hummingbirds

these blossoms   the color of
all the anger you have ever known
puckered ruffs couching
dim   green hearts

the seed packet boasted
butterflies   said nothing of
gorgeous   slick flowers
reminiscent of aftershock

color left
in the wake of pain

Telegram

spring   so they will bring word to you
the farm clamped down in gumbo
five dark miles from the highway
ditches running deep
to flood & nourish the poplar spears

what the war taught you
that there is no good in these missives
how you watched your mother's life
unpicked by panic   fretwork of pattern
blown like cobweb
such possibility
lodged in that slim envelope
wedged between the stops

little wonder your hand
quakes upon receipt
tips the teapot cock-eyed
over stoneware   you blot
the spill with a shirtsleeve   feel
fear cauterize reason   slit
the flap before nerves desert

your wife is doing well
   coming home when
   the roads open up
bringing the baby

from the hill   you watch
the back forty gone to muskeg
& tamarack   the shifting dance of
slough birds   white pelican lifts
a pleated wing
to steer out over dark water
navigating the skin of things

these still   black places
this accidental light

Wild Onions

creek ducks the boundary fence
leaves it slackjawed & dangling
spring   the cattle
wallow in runoff mud
play their spines along the wire

up the coulee
ironstone peters to cactus
wild lupine

the onions are found
by scent   bite
of trodden leaves
    bulbs unearthed like molars
    crepuscular canyon light

wild taste of
earth & dark water

coyote on a lip of land   ochre
moon saddling predawn sky

Small Deaths

Doulton china
a brass bell &
five broken mattocks
    knocked headless in *caliche*
    brickhard red clay

at the foot of the lilacs
a cracked headstone
small grave pickaxed clear

the mattocks tell a new story

I-nis'kim

1.

first   the farmsteads
slip under
to wind or   drought
      spring clapboard warping
      lichen like sparrowprint

towns taken   gradually
limb by limb   feed & tackle
dry goods   when the
post office goes it's done for

takes years   though   before
the church windows vanish
      someone brave or
      desperate enough
& then scrapboard blinkers
bell tower gone to pigeons

2.

what the posters showed
        wheat   & sky
the bushel bins
full to overflowing

reality
high summer   Battleford
        cyclonic dust &
        missing chinks
grit a constant partner

standing   she raises
her hem from the floor
leaves a perfect negative of
bleached pine

he   hawks dust   polishes
the flintlock & hangs it
above the door

all day
the brightness goes out of it
like a veiled eye

3.

two days ago
he loaded the rifle   palmed
his way along the storm line
to the barn

inside   five roans
lean & hard as oak

   in the kitchen   she laid the table
   turned plates like white moons

incendiary sunset   the horses
wild & rank with fear
scenting death   powder

rifle not for them

for him

4.

in front of the house   the yard
gives way to prairie grass
          fescue & grama
distantly   the church
knuckles under like an old woman
steeple sloughed & rotting

she finds it
nestled in a pucker of earth
          slim   pale rock
              imbued with kingfisher light

I-nis'kim   buffalo stone

promise of plenty when
the town has gone   the church
down to staves

*pray that you will not starve
& the buffalo will come*

sun in weals over napped ground
stunted barley

you will not starve

come

          pray

Harvest

what turns up is not
always what we expect

among the new potatoes
cranberry glass   sharded
porcelain   the banded trunks
rattling like teeth in steerage &
England's vanishing coast
a fond green smear

in the kitchen garden
a necklace restrings itself
gradually   thirties silver
grubbed from this mingy soil

what sort of epitaph in
these thin   bright droplets
soil turned beyond powder
   foundation stones in this garden
   refusing to give way
   go down

Legend, 1942

saskatchewan in autumn
war & harvest
fields given over to
air bases

times like these
where you come from less important than
how strong your shoulders
& how willing

& your name
falling unnoticed in
the wake of the threshing crew

heritage here
in the hands
   scythe in churchyard grass   the arc
   of axe & mattock

this land's bones
too stubborn for words

Lesson, St. Boswells

that geese will return
for grain & the dugout
long after the bubble gas pumps
rust through   glass caps lost
to children & stones

that pigeons will move in
from the elevator vault &
prairie crocus from   everywhere

that what builds a town
can kill it   the swingarm
of economy & how
grass still lips at the railbed
    tongue playing at
    spaces

    this stolen language

lepidopterists

What form of mysterious pursuit caused me to get my feet

wet like a child, to pant up a talus, to stare every dandelion in

the face, to start at every coloured mote passing just beyond

my field of vision? What was the dream sensation of having

come empty-handed — without what? A gun? A wand?

VLADIMIR NABOKOV

Lintel

prairie station
planked against horizon line

train pulls out   leaves
you   & her
scrying flanker hieroglyphics
in trackside snow

spring
burns across this landscape
long after you had hoped
   somehow   before you were ready
coaxes
butterflies   almost overnight
from drying patches
of muddy ground

teaches you this

waning hoop of moon
aped by your net's cirque

summer
a riot of gypsy wings

lone oil lamp
in the window

   she draws you
   roving
       home

Mary Norton

1708–1728

Country wife of explorer Samuel Hearne
Starved to death near Prince of Wales Fort, Churchill, Manitoba
Winter 1728

Riding's Satyr

(W.H. Edwards, 1865)

several shades of brown
she is tucked against bare earth
when you find her

& blue grama bright
on parched soil

flight like a grasshopper
she hits the ground
running

Mary

skyline a weatherglass
thick with portent

the country wives squat
to shuck corn
blonde silk catching
at their fingers

Nellie McClung

1873–1951

From a sixteen-year-old schoolteacher in Manitou, Manitoba to one of the Famous Five who changed forever women's place in the West

Gray Copper

(Scudder, 1869)

waste field burled
with milkweed   thick fastness of
silk tufts

she dangles limp
from battered shingles
   stilldamp body
   flagging the wind

shanty windows
punched out
standing blindside to
its lengthening shadow

farmstead a susurrus of
silver down   quickening wings

Nellie

what the women know

    that two things alter the face
    of man   & prairie

arid june days   a bellows of
cyclone dust & stripling wheat

grass fire along the shelterbelt   how
cottonwoods in august
kindle like tallow

prairie knows the right of it
where you are is where you stand

The Wives of Crowfoot

1830–1890

By the time of the signing of Treaty 7
Crowfoot had had up to ten wives in his household

Many of their names have been lost to time

Afranius Duskywing

(Lintner, 1878)

unremarkable
she rests amongst
the buffalo bean

   what is slight
   goes unnoticed

hush of two generations
finding flight
lapis wings
bluing the air

Crowfoot's Wives

Cutting Woman   *Sisoyaki*
sits-beside-him-wife
watches
this man wither

one son mute   one blind
ten wives & only four children
grown
    three daughters

what the new language means
    this peace tongue
diphtheria
tuberculosis
how he lives through them all
    marked
    reluctant witness

smallpox
whiskey

Sisoyaki
Nipistaiaki
Ayistsi
Sowki-pi-aki
Awatoht-sinik
Pi-ot-skini
Asinaki

& three
never named

Manitupotis' Women

1873

Cypress Hills
Southern Alberta floundering under the whiskey trade
Several members of the band led by Manitupotis
(Little Soldier) and his band massacred by American wolfers

Arrowhead Blue

(Boisduval, 1852)

the lupines' bloom
stills at dusk

all day   they have thrust
silvery-purple against
the hills' spine
their scent
tearing the air like clamour

angling her wings
she dips amongst
violent petals
    patina the depth
    of a new bruise
a perennial ache

Nakoda Woman

Cypress Hills, 1873

*'Lupinus' is taken from lupus, 'wolf,' because of a belief
that these plants destroy the soul.*
TRICIA POLLOCK

the wolfers brought the massacre

she observed it from the scrub
wary of those who fight wolves
by not fighting

    strychnine
    incendiary in the buffalo carcasses

what hope   then
for men so far gone in
shame &   drink

& these flowers
    wild lupines
a scent
pervasive as guilt

unforgiving as memory

Margaret Fleming

1901–1999

Double life:
School teacher and single woman in Winnipeg, Manitoba
Mountaineer in Banff and Jasper, editor of the Canadian
Alpine Journal

Mariposa Copper

(Reakirt, 1866)

tawny
flint of flight

she lives
in a brighter hue

knotweed spun
with nimble
salem wings

Margaret

heights caught
at something like
soul

nine mountains
in thirty days

& a new world
opening like language

buttress chimney
deadman cramped in snow

how they hauled
her slim weight
over summit
after summit
dodging adamantine glare

seeing only
this avian woman
   bones clamped
   to mountain
   by sheer will

on the *glissade*
down burnished ice

her gasp
tore free
the delight
from your own throat

Dr. Elizabeth Beckett Matheson

1866–1958

From teacher in Manitoba
to doctor in northern Saskatchewan

Thousands of miles cross-country
offering help to isolated settlements

Jutta Arctic

(Hübner, 1806)

she is a thread of light
among the tamaracks   her flight
cutting the crossweave
of muskeg green

the labrador tea
fascinates   leaves curling
hirsute bellies in ochre & emerald

thinlipped blossoms
opaque as antler
fragrant with moss
& sun

Elizabeth

trust
is gained in miles

summer peat bogs
spicy with rot   &
corduroy roads
pitching under the horses
        as though even the land
        would cast you off

this work
a new kind of medicine

a people learned
through the earth &
its ways of healing
        wild blueberry
        elder
bitter willow bark tea

waking to travel
wild hours at night
the land opens you
maskihkiwiskwew

a woman who heals

alone in a logging wagon
under coyote moon

the home place

Cairns

lessons in returning
    willow & alder flats by the river
    in spring gumbo

how you come back to a place
at the vestiges of memory

these sullen old planks   joists
pushing at the skin
    mice in the cistern &
    the wellwater flat & green

bring pebbles
fumbled into pockets
at every place you have ever left
    as if what holds us here
    could be won this blindly

bring canyon sandstone
bright malicious obsidian   bring
dimestore quartzes
perhaps diamonds
    robbed of newlywed sheen
    cauled & grey as crones' eyes

bring them   here
lay them sidewise along
foundation lines   wait
for the brittle tongue of memory

only stone speaks
to stone

Farmhouse, Castor

early sun skims
the plate rail   a kitchen
reduced to grit & shambles
    butcherblock table
      wallpaper slumped about its knees

light here reveals
only   absence

teasel in the bones of
the victory garden   thrusting
barrel staves like iron ribs

what we have come for

lilacs pressing in
these diamond panes   their blossom
stark & fragrant across the hearth
    rainwater shifting in
      the stair's curved spine

how this land holds everything &
nothing   back

Called Back

(In Memoriam, G. Johnson)

they left Dorothy in the 30s
   tailspin of the Dustbowl
   farm sunk under rabbitbrush
hitched farther west

successive babies
slung precariously at her back   they drove
cattle   worked the threshing crews
retired to a northern city

      more dark water than
      they'd ever seen   & thinlimbed pines

& now
eighty-five   dodging Alzheimer's
he brings her south again
to finish where he started

she scours the porch
at the seniors' residence
   thinks forty years of northern spruce
   slimwillow loon-call

nothing to fasten on here but
claretcup   paintbrush
sunbruised petals she spots & loves hard

Forestfire, Waterton

liminal magnetism of
these hills   how
grasslands broadside rock
with schooner gait

this morning
the crags rise
red as smoked glass

    frantic counterpoint of orioles

Locusts, Milk River

summer   we pitch
our tents on the bluffs
coarse sand beach measured
in winterwhite limbs

each night
a heat lightning sky
& the bats vaulting
updrafts over the water

at nine   you watch
the teens pair off
nip whiskey from a battered flask
smelling of tobacco
somebody's grandfather

what you will remember
    how locusts sound like rain
    hatching out of too-dry ground

ride the girls shrieking
into the river

August

summer is two mickeys &
Vancouver weed
riding the pumpjacks at dawn

& how you can hop a train
to the coast if you're daring
high or   maybe a little crazy
    this insouciant sun &
    the nights bigger than
    we could have dreamed

how the days are   bullion
    hot & salt   our bodies
the crushed pockets in tall grass
behind the scrapyard fence
as if deer had wintered there

the way heat eases &
pummels a town
when the elevators fall   when
we are faced with
the rubble of their passing

emptied nests under the ridgeline
this &   the thin night's leavings

Hobby Farmer

less about grain than
the slim thighs of land
lost to drought   sculpted
by hard weather
& how to explain to your wife
the rich dark stir
of spring earth

she   circumscribed in
the domestic
   geraniums
     crocus corms like knucklebones

& what you lack

a means to say
I would give it all for
one night on this land
smudged like guilt into palmlines

how the light turns
at dusk & in autumn
& how   always
out here I know where I stand

Vigil, Estevan

what must be watched for

blind feeder roots on
the geraniums in the cellar
   this   more than anything on
   winter's outward crawl

first parsnips   the thin
red haze of duststorm
wildfire   cottonwoods
weighted down with orioles

& the way
light hunkers over the old thresher
rusting into earth
out on the east quarter
   this blue & that
   viridian night arc of sky

hawks that follow
the combine swath &
spindles of crows in
unrelieved black

baler faltering to silence
on the back forty
   how panic thrums like wings

Ghost Town Ghazal

snow whimpers in the lees   air smelling
of spring   furrows greening

slivers of bottleglass   fragmented slough ice
willow glyph against sky

in the abandoned farm garden
a penumbra of red tulips

barn swallows know the heft of leaving
doorway linteled with light

what falls & how
the far horizon ,   this rain

Reunion

Robinhood, 1991

as if one phone call could
fend off the ghosts

coming into town
pickup shunting like a heifer
through the potholes
thinking you've done it
    bunting lapping at the church eaves
    grass lopped & bundled &
    ubiquitous ham sandwiches
that double for weddings & funerals

if collective wishful thinking
could backcrank the clock
    it'd look like this

church shimmying free of
encroaching poplars   sidewalks flush &
fences cinching in spraddled pickets
& the dance floor
the way it used to be

bluegrass &   cheek to cheek

Seven Ways of Leaving

1.

four a.m.   when
early red bludgeons
the canyon out of dark

old truck beetling along
the access road as though
there were more to this than
one empty cup drying
beside the sink
    thin china   bonewhite
    & chased with sun

2.

the way
frost releases a pane
center first

what is left
clings to the frame
a rime of crystals on metal
    beauty resident in structure
    something about the bones

3.

when the wheat came down
how the mice closed
in centripetal flight
    redtailed hawks delineating
    the combine swath
yes   like that

4.

yearling wolf out in the grass
& even you reluctant
to bring your rifle

on the canyon rim
cattle knot   scatter &
how the bullet loops
a low arc
out across the sagebrush

what is remembered
the wolf's legs   limber sun
those long   racing shadows

5.

because marriage is less
about rings than
spirals   the fretworked granary floor
when the cats have been in

moonhued garden snails
plucked & dropped into
saltwater   dim reprimand of
shells against the bucket's tin

       you take home with you
       when you go

6.

more to this than we think

magpies hounding off
the last unsuspecting owl

sun shamed into rising

7.

either side of the tracks
grainsheds shoulder
each other's eaves

when the trucks pull out
houses gain
a shiftiness
this slackkneed patience
ridgelined with pigeons

how two winters
can flagellate siding
to aluminum sheen

ruins coruscating like signal lights
long after the tracks have gone

Alchemist

Writing-On-Stone Provincial Park, 1999

the irony is
I come into being when called
   bucking like Sisyphus this
   unloved summoning

your voice
the wind   polytonal over
one stone or another

I come   & with me
earth   incarnadine &
toothsome
   musk   dog rose
   bramble
things that
flaunt & catch

petals
thorns

what name
for a shambles of
meat & strings

the wind playing over
my mouth a riveted
O

glass   firmament

I breathe & am

Tawayik

(Stopping Place)

here   once
night camps
    these hills
    respite from prairie

how time works
    blurs along sightline

fingering boundaries
pumpjacks in hackneyed dance

sojourners now
october geese
their horizon cries

& over refineries
    steadily thumbing their way north
thin bone talon
of the hawking moon

The Home Place

(for Les & Laura Tywoniuk)

last quarter
sells late autumn

agent dares
the small hospital
    triage   one ward
      pinioned against north country

how to say
in this room
with its fallowfield view

that there is no going back

on the quarter
tundra swans fringe the creek
one afternoon only
    gone at dusk on
    supernatural wings

lone bed on the ward
old farmer
butterflied in traction
steelpinned against flight
    against return

do not breathe here
so much could shatter

The Sea Cave

I am two weeks off a prairie sky
reluctant islander   what I don't know of
spring & neap

urchin barrens denuded of green
how you laugh at my bafflement
night-swimming the bay   spooned in phosphorescence

your casual negotiation of
basalt's black tongue   limbs of beaches
kelp-sleek   slattern with sea

at dusk   you show me
gifts stolen from the shore   moon snails
bottle glass in submerged shades   the slick

dark mouth of the sea cave footing the jetty
& noon   how I scream when
you ride the waves against that shelf

the sea cave gathering you in
no hollow in my knowing for the boom of tide
like pulse in such a space

& you emerge like Sedna on
an outrider wave   untouched
as though the earth's heart is known to you

is quiescent as grassland   easily shed
as salt brushed
from drying skin

Trapline

The greatest beauty is to be alive, forgetting nothing,
although remembrance hurts
like a foolish act, is a foolish act.
JOHN NEWLOVE

nights closing on themselves already
this north country
burnishing its bones one against the other
August slinks her limber spine
protests aspen on the turn
haptic shingling of frost on birch

in the muskeg spruce
we scout snare points   memorize
the fall of light and timber
plan returns in snow
to stretch steel jaws
pound anchor chains

when you taught me
about killing   I learned
how little keeps us
    how to bleed out in the bush
    and walk through fiercely
    as though unshaken

something in us
wound with the season
summer's hollowing cheeks   the snap
of knucklebones

gather me up and cast

         winter oracle

Alberta, 1983

(for my mother)

she is still young enough
to remember the bougainvillea
on the eaves   old men
shuffling in the breezeway
   how paan dyes the teeth
   red &   black
   those rictus grins

at three   my scope
a different sort of internal

this prairie
leaves her hollow   her hands
riffling the spice cupboard
for turmeric   cardamom
& the sari silks
preserved like butterflies

how a cedar trunk can be
big enough to hold a world
   Dar-Es-Salaam   its blossoms
   & fragrance

& that a seven-month cold spell
limns the bones

what she taught us:
sparrow's endurance in ice-blind trees
bone rattle of memory & winter

Seldom Seen Road

what is true about this land

that prairie is scant
but wears it well
    snowdrifts slung like mink

that all signs last
grasslands a skein of bruises
wagon trails &
retreating bluestem

& that   against earth
everything is transitory
soddies & clapboard
railbed sown under

sun catches your eye like
a backward glance

alights   moves on

AUTHOR'S NOTES

The title "Victory Garden" comes from the food, flower, and herb gardens encouraged by the governments of the United States, Canada, and the United Kingdom during World Wars I and II. The gardens were designed to remove some of the demand for food from already scanty national supplies, as well as to boost morale amongst the people by allowing them to contribute to their home country's war efforts.

"I-nis'kim" is a sacred Blackfoot medicine object, often a small stone of unusual colour or a fossilized shell. Sometimes thought to resemble an animal in shape, the I-nis'kim, or Buffalo Stone, was once used in a ritual for calling back the buffalo in times of starvation. The poem makes mention of the Buffalo Stone to highlight this lack of spiritual connection to the land in the narrative of the incoming settlers.

"Lepidopterists": This section connects women of historical importance on the prairies to butterflies from the same geographic area that were discovered approximately within the corresponding woman's lifetime. The series is an homage to those stereotypically considered frail — women and butterflies — that both played such key roles in the history of the West. Basic information about the characteristics and discovery dates of the various butterflies was gleaned from the excellent website http://www.cbif.gc.ca/spp_pages/butterflies/geography_e.php

"Reunion, Robinhood, 1991" refers to the town of Robinhood, Saskatchewan. Declared a ghost town when its post office closed down in 1971, the community came back to life for one day in 1991, when the grandson of two of the town's inhabitants returned home to marry his sweetheart. Over 100 people congregated in the town's church for the wedding and attended the festivities in the community hall afterward. But, Cinderella-like, the spell cast over Robinhood lasted only a day. The community resumed its slump into anonymity, and once again, few people live there today. ("The Church," from Johnnie Bachusky's Guardian of the Ghosts project. www.nobleghosts.com)

"Tawayik" means "halfway" in Cree. At one point in its history, Tawayik Lake was a resting area for Cree bands travelling between hunting camps in the Beaver Hills and Fort Edmonton. It is now part of Elk Island Provincial Park.

ACKNOWLEDGEMENTS

Several of these poems have appeared or will appear in the following publications: *CV2, Grain, The Rialto, The Goose (Journal of the Association for Literature, the Environment, and Culture in Canada),* and *blueskiespoetry.com;* the anthologies *Poems From Planet Earth, Writing the Land: Alberta Through Its Poets, Home and Away,* and *A Verdant Green;* and the chapbooks *Winter Ballast* (The Olive Reading Series 2008) and *Lepidopterists* (stately/Plump Publishing, forthcoming). "Telegram" was the winning entry in CV2's 2-Day Poem Contest (2006). *Seldom Seen Road* was listed as one of the top three manuscripts in CV2's Show Me the Book Contest 2009.

A great debt of gratitude is owed to the following wonderful people, without whom this collection would not exist: Les & Laura Tywoniuk, for the home place; Denise Riley and George Szirtes, for long faith in these poems; Robert Kroetsch, in memory of kindness as vast as the prairie sky; and Doug Barbour, as always.

Jenna Butler was born in Norwich, England, close to
the North Sea. Her family emigrated to Canada in the early eighties,
initially moving to Toronto and finally settling in Alberta. The sense
of belonging to, and simultaneously not quite fitting into, two places
— England and Canada — has heavily influenced her work, which
often focuses on the varied landscapes of these two countries.

Butler holds BA and B.Ed degrees from the University of Alberta, in
addition to an MA and PhD in Creative and Critical Writing from
the University of East Anglia (UK). She is the author of two previous
trade books of poetry, *Aphelion* (NeWest Press, 2010) and *Wells*
(University of Alberta Press, 2012), as well as ten short collections
with small presses in Canada, the United States, and Europe.

Butler teaches Literature and Creative Writing at Grant MacEwan
University and divides her time between Edmonton, England, and
the small farm she runs with her husband in Alberta's north country.

"Jenna Butler brings a fresh set of eyes and a startling lyric language to these poems, a wonderful re-imagining of these prairies and of the people whose stories are part of our history. One of her narrators declares, "always/out here I know where I stand" and Butler's poems ring with the same conviction."

GLEN SORESTAD
author of *Leaving Holds Me Here*

"*Seldom Seen Road* dances readers to new ways of knowing; glimpses of the remarkable but often unremarked shadow sides of beauty and pain oscillate with grace and verve. Jenna Butler's fine eye and ear are the best of companions."

BARBARA LANGHORST
author of *Restless White Fields*

www.newestpress.com

ISBN 1-927063-31-0

9 781927 063316

$14.95